Dear Mei Mei —

Hope you can use this book to figure me out ... haha!

Love,
Mom
'28/07

How to
Read
People
Like a book

**50 Uncommon Tips
You Need to Know**

MURRAY OXMAN

SOURCEBOOKS, INC.®
NAPERVILLE, ILLINOIS

Published by Sourcebooks, Inc.
P.O. Box 4410, Naperville, Illinois   60567-4410
(630) 961-3900
Fax: (630) 961-2168
www.sourcebooks.com

Originally published in 2002

Library of Congress Cataloging-in-Publication Data
Oxman, Murray.
  How to read people like a book : 50 uncommon tips you need to know /
Murray Oxman.
    p. cm.
  Originally published: United States : Success Without Stress, 2002.
  ISBN-13: 978-1-4022-0693-1
  ISBN-10: 1-4022-0693-3
  1. Personality assessment--Miscellanea. 2. Body language. I. Title.

BF698.4.O96 2006
158.2--dc22

                                                    2006008206

Printed and bound in the United States of America.
            LB   10 9 8 7 6 5 4 3 2 1

This book is most humbly dedicated to the
Truth that sets us free.

Introduction

Please picture in your mind some people wandering in a scorched desert, dying of thirst. Then, as if by magic, a beautiful oasis appears a few yards ahead of them, complete with a clean, clear pool of water.

Most of the wanderers are suspicious and say things like, "It's a trick. The water is surely not fit to drink. It will kill us." They wander off into the desert and certain death. But one couple, a man and a woman, decide not to go with the others. Their reasoning is, "Wait a minute, wandering in the desert for one more day will surely kill us. This water looks and smells clean. And there's even dates on those trees over there!" Soon the couple had quenched their thirst and eaten their fill of dates. Two days later they were rescued by a search party sent to find them.

Like the beautiful oasis, Truth is always waiting and willing to help any and all. But, it never forces anyone to drink of its life-saving water. We must want it. Let's go to work right now.

I would like to most respectfully suggest that you read this book at least three times. The first time to casually familiarize yourself with the writing style and content. A second reading aloud to oneself is an amazing tool for deeper understanding of any subject you want to delve into. I think you will discover important points you missed in the first reading. The third reading will reveal even more helpful points and a further understanding of the subject of reading people. Remember the guides are not about us feeling superior to others and finding fault. They are about each of us achieving a better understanding of human nature—including our own. Or to put it another way: to help to smooth out the bumps in the road of life.

Chapters One through Fifty are helpful guides. Chapter Fifty-One is made up of interesting questions and answers from a class on reading people in Corvallis, Oregon. These questions and answers are referred to for further insights into a particular guide. You'll see a notation like this: ** See questions and answers 4 and 18.

1

Trading

People can be very manipulative, and trading is a big part of it. They will appear very sincere in supporting your ideas and/or actions—but they expect something in return for their support: They want you to support what they are doing. Never trade with people. Stand on your own two feet. Once people catch on that you can't be bought they'll show their true colors. Then they are very easy to read and understand.

** See questions and answers 3, 13, and 14.

2

Honesty

Remember an honest person does not feel threatened when questioned about his intentions. If he starts the "What's the matter, you don't trust me?" routine, don't answer. Just keep asking your questions. He will quickly reveal what he is—dishonest!

** See question and answer 22.

3

Approval

There are people who beg for approval. It may or may not be in words. It could be in a gesture or in their eyes. Why do they seek your approval? They don't want to be self-responsible or self-reliant. You cause harm to the other person and to yourself when you let them lean on you. Yes, there is a momentary thrill of false power when you are asked to approve of someone, but it actually makes everyone involved weak. When you refuse that momentary thrill, you always feel the rightness of it. Your heart smiles.

** See question and answer 21.

4

Flattery

We all quickly and easily recognize flattery when someone else is on the receiving end. But when the flatterer is spreading it on thick for us, it is much harder to catch. Be aware. When someone starts feeding your ego, ask yourself, "Just what is he after—do I want to go along with this?"

** See question and answer 25.

5

Standard

A married couple, in their late thirties, had moved to a small town to escape big city life. After getting settled in their new surroundings, they started noticing the people about town. There was one older man who particularly interested them. They inquired about him and were most often told, "He moved here several years ago…don't know where he's from. The best way to describe him is—he's different."

One bright, sunny day the couple was taking a walk on the local beach. They spied the old man of interest not far away. They approached the man with a big smile and a warm "hello." He returned their warm smiles and said, "Nice day."

"Mind if we walk with you and talk?" asked the young man. "Not at all," replied the older man, "Glad to have a little company." "We were wondering about something…" the young couple said in unison. "Yes?" asked the man. "You always seem so cheerful, relaxed, really happy—content," the young lady commented. She continued, "Most people you meet these days are tight as a violin string. They don't look very happy. What's your secret? If you have one."

The older man smiled a big smile and said, "The two of you are very observant. My secret is a simple one. When I was quite a bit younger I often noticed that, in everything, people had a higher standard for others than they had for themselves. For a long time I didn't know what to do with this bit of human psychology I had observed. Then one day, something I had read many years earlier popped up in my head. It was an instruction a Mystic Master had said his much beloved maternal grandmother had given him when he was a boy: 'In everything, never do as others do.' For the first time, I understood what that instruction meant. From that moment on, I always set the standard for my actions above what I expected from others. Plus, I always raised the present standard for myself. That's it. There you have my secret for a life that is always nice and pleasant." The three of them continued their leisurely stroll along the beach. The young couple smiled inwardly for they knew they had learned a Great Truth.

** See questions and answers 2 and 7.

6

Rushing

Have you had an encounter with the kind of person who appears to be going a thousand miles an hour? And they want you to go as fast as they are. Maybe they want you to make a snap decision on an important matter—right now. Don't get caught up in their momentum. Deliberately slow down! You dictate the tempo that things will move. Always and in everything, be your own person.

** See questions and answers 11 and 28.

Eyes

Whether you're speaking with or looking at a picture of someone, be sure to look at their eyes. They reveal a lot. Recently there was a picture of a famous actor on the cover of a magazine. He had a big smile on his face, but his eyes told a completely different story. They were full of pain, resentment, and defeat. When engaged in a conversation, notice if the person avoids or seeks eye contact with you. People who are hiding something usually avoid eye contact. Some even wear sunglasses because they know their eyes will betray them. Honest people do not avoid eye contact.

** See questions and answers 3 and 4.

8

Actors

The person who proclaims they are this or that kind of person isn't. For instance, a person may declare, "I'm very open-minded." You can bet on it—this is a very closed individual. They actually believe they are open because they play the role so well. In reality they can only fool other pretenders.

** See question and answer 19.

9

Birds of a Feather

In nature you never see the aggressive hawk and the cooing dove associating. Why? Two very different temperaments. Natural law separates the two. The same law applies to people. Two people might appear very different on the surface, but below the surface be birds of a feather.

** See question and answer 5.

10

Insecurity

Insecure people want everyone to dress as they do, think as they do, feel as they do, and speak as they do (of course they copied everything from someone else). If you don't, they immediately label you. Want your own life? Let them call you whatever they want to call you. It's a small price to pay for your individuality.

** See question and answer 20.

11

Helpless

"Please help me make this decision. I just don't know what to do." Those words are always an invitation to an unhappy situation. Here are three reasons not to give people advice:

First, they most likely will not take it anyway.

Second, woe be unto you if you do and it doesn't work out well. You will forever be reminded of your mistake.

Third, and worst of all, even if things work out, you still lose. The hapless, helpless person will never stop asking you for advice.

You might consider this reply when people ask you for advice: "The best advice I can give you, if you don't know what to do, is—do nothing!"

** See questions and answers 1 and 10.

Thank You

Quite often when someone tells you, "Thank you!" what they really mean is, "Please do it again." Be careful not to fall for the lure of wanting people to like you and giving them gifts to ensure that they do.

** See questions and answers 19 and 21.

Please Yourself

Trying to please others will get you nothing but anxiety, nervousness, and scorn. Please your True Self and you receive the inner-riches of a nice, relaxed, confident life.

** See questions and answers 9 and 24.

14

Feeling Sad

Some people get a false thrill out of feeling sorry for themselves. Plus they want others to join in by feeling sorry for them as well. Feeling sorry and feeling bad are one and the same. Neither does anything but cause pain and suffering. Don't get drawn into this trap. Cheerfulness is a healthy alternative.

** See questions and answers 1, 6, and 28.

15

Responsibility

There are lots of people who want to avoid all personal responsibilities. They want others to think for them, do their work for them, pay their bills for them, etc. The nice and helpful thing you can do for this type of person is to refuse to help him. Throw him back upon himself. It teaches self-reliance and builds character—which truly helps him. Helping him any other way only weakens and harms him.

** See questions and answers 10 and 15.

16

Special

People like to feel special. What's shocking is what they will do to feel special. For instance, people will conjure up in their minds how they think life and everyone on the planet should treat them. If life and everyone doesn't treat them this way, they feel hurt, depressed, resentful, or some other equally painful emotion. They believe their self-inflicted pain makes them someone special. People who want to be special are harmful to themselves and others.

** See question and answer 25.

Friends

Sadly, it is human nature to gravitate to those people who tell you what you want to hear. However, people who tell you what you want to hear do so for a reason—they want something from you. That is not friendship—it's exploitation. A real friend will always tell you what you need to hear—the Truth—not what you prefer to hear. To put it another way, Truth is really the only friend a person can have and needs. Friends in Truth are real friends.

** See question and answer 3.

Cupid

When Cupid is hovering about, ready to shoot his arrows, both men and women tend to put only their best foot forward. As we all can attest, the person you thought you were getting involved with in no way resembles the person you're ultimately paired with. Solution: Drop the image! Never play a role! Be yourself! Now you will be able to separate the false from the real in others.

** See questions and answers 4 and 18.

19

Comfort

Human beings are driven by the desire for comfort. Always remember when you're dealing with anyone that if you say or do anything that threatens their sense of comfort, you'll have a fight on your hands. Don't push people psychologically. They'll resist and push back. Use tact, slow down, take your time, and introduce new ideas to them gradually, so they'll feel at ease with you.

** See question and answer 23.

Lies

Once a person lies to you, you can expect it will happen again. Not that the person can't change, but most don't want to change. They would even rather lie when the truth would serve them far better. Best bet: have nothing to do with liars!

** See questions and answers 10 and 26.

21

Events

When life presents people with an unfavorable event, most complain that life or maybe God is against them. They feel that others have advantages. The Truth is, we all attract every event in our lives. What we attract is determined by who we are—our nature. Anyone can change their life, anytime they choose, by simply changing their nature.

** See question and answer 2.

Free

Everyone likes to get something for nothing. There are people who have learned how to manipulate individuals and/or the system to get a free ride in life. Individuals give handouts to these people to enhance their own image as a "caring person." Politicians give handouts to buy votes. There really are no free lunches, as the old saying goes. Anything of real value costs something. When anyone gives unearned benefits to another, both the giver and the taker are harmed—each suffers from their false feeling of superiority.

** See question and answer 21.

Baggage

People carry a lot of unnecessary psychological baggage—resentment, hurt, depression—you name it! This baggage causes terrible psychological pain. This self-induced hell makes people mean. Many are very practiced at putting on a mask of sweetness and niceness, but the meanness is always there under the surface. Be very careful when getting involved with anyone, whether it be in your personal life or business—they might be a human volcano. Never be afraid to see things the way they are, even if it's frightening at first.

** See questions and answers 8 and 15.

24

Environment

Correctly so, people are concerned with the health of our natural environment. However, what could be more important than our own psychological and spiritual environment? Yet, few are concerned. There is never a right, healthy time to feel bad. Cheerfulness is a nice, healthy environment. People who spread pollution with their gloomy spirit should be avoided. They will pollute your spirit.

** See questions and answers 6, 12, and 17.

Priorities

You can tell a lot about people by observing what their priorities are. Not what they say they are, but what you observe them to actually be. Then after observing, decide if he or she is the kind of person you want to associate with.

** See question and answer 9.

26

Wants

Everyone senses when another person wants something from them—whatever it is. It can make us feel special, especially if we are attracted to that person. But here's the catch: People who want something from you are generally after only what they desire. Once they get it, they leave—physically or psychologically. Is it worth the price you have to pay for feeling flattered because someone wants something from you? No!

** See question and answer 22.

Protection

The next time you are with a group of people, sit quietly and observe them. Notice how everyone is doing their best to protect what we call "myself." Notice how the act of "protecting" causes anxiety, nervousness, and pain. We have been doing it for so long, we do not even notice it. Lesson: Drop the "protection" and you automatically drop its running mates—anxiety, nervousness, and pain.

** See questions and answers 8 and 20.

Answers

*

Have you ever noticed that when you ask some people questions, you rarely get a straight answer? They are either vague or have nothing to do with the question at hand. Don't hesitate to repeat the question until you get a direct answer. Or, when you get vague, rambling answers ask, "Exactly, what does that mean?"

** See question and answer 27.

Trust

If you really consider it, trusting anyone, even ourselves, doesn't make sense. If we trust, we don't watch, we take things for granted, we get lazy, and we miss a lot. But if we watch everything and everyone with a sense of inquisitiveness, we remain alert and fresh. No, this doesn't mean to be distrustful and paranoid—just do not trust—watch! Try it and then decide for yourself which is the better approach.

** See question and answer 18.

30

Relax

In your daily routine interactions with people, nothing could be more helpful to all concerned than to relax! (Even if you have to force yourself.)

** See question and answer 11.

Power

There is nothing that delights people of weak character more than having false power over others. They love to cause other people problems and grief—the more the better. They thrive on eliciting negative reactions from anyone. Far too frequently we must deal with this type of lost person. The key: Remember they watch for a negative reaction. If you have one, don't express it. Bear it consciously. (Factually, the pain we feel isn't caused by the other person's actions. It's caused by our own negative reaction. It's a mechanical reaction carried over unconsciously from the past and really has nothing to do with the incident at hand. Giving in to it gives it more power. But, bearing negative reactions consciously and not expressing them leads to being totally free of them.)

** See question and answer 12.

Accountability

Now there's a not-too-often used word these days. Most people are primed and ready to go with a backpack of excuses for every misstep they make. They immediately plead, "I'm the victim, the person harmed. I never hurt anyone. I'm really being misunderstood here." It is interesting to note that we humans often miss the obvious: No one ever gets away with anything. The instant we harm another person, we also harm ourselves. People who hold themselves accountable are to be admired. They make for good company—others do not!

** See question and answer 15.

Questions

Maybe you have already noticed that people will ask questions, but almost never listen to the answers. Why? They are only interested in answers that confirm their way of looking at things. If the answer challenges anything about them, the wall goes up instantly. Of course, they will swear they really want to learn and are all ears. They most likely will be able to quote what was said to them word for word, but they never really heard a thing.

** See question and answer 10.

34

Individuality

Once upon a time there was a flock of sheep grazing on a beautiful hillside of dark green grass in Utah. One fine day, one of the newly matured male sheep looked about and noticed that all the sheep looked alike—"No individuality," he thought to himself. He taxed his brain trying to come up with something he could do to make him feel more like an individual and less like all the other sheep. Over an hour went by before the answer he was looking for appeared in his sheepish brain. His brain reminded him of a huge bull, with a ring in his nose, he had seen one time. He instantly liked the idea of looking like a huge, strong bull instead of a small sheepish sheep. He bleated and pleaded with the shepherd until he finally got the nose ring he so badly wanted. Now he was an individual—not like the other sheep. At first all the other sheep laughed at our hero, but after listening to his explanation about individuality, their brains started to change tunes: "Maybe he has something there," they thought. Would you believe it? No more than a month went by before all the sheep on the beautiful green hillside in Utah were munching grass with rings in their noses.

Real individuality does exist. It is always natural. It is never contrived. It cannot be acquired. It is there right now, waiting to be discovered by any brave soul who is willing to get rid of everything he has accumulated that is not part of his natural individuality.

** See questions and answers 9 and 25.

35

Pain

Have you ever heard someone moan something like this? "What a day, the stress was terrible, now I can relax a little." Don't buy it! It's a self-centered act to feel important and get a false sense of accomplishment. People wrongly equate suffering with accomplishment. The two have absolutely nothing in common: Stress, anxiety, and painful emotional reactions are all self-induced. It's all part of the self-centeredness that we all have bought into. People will wish one another a nice day but will not give themselves one. All it takes is giving up our self-centeredness by noticing how much it hurts.

** See question and answer 18.

Heroes

Empty human beings seek a false feeling of self through identifying with false heroes. One must never identify with anyone or anything. There have been real heroes on this planet, but they had nothing to do with sports, social causes, or entertainment. J. Krishnamurti and Vernon Howard were true modern heroes—spiritual heroes. Even though their books were read by millions of people, they remain relatively unknown.

** See questions and answers 5 and 7.

Procrastination

Here's a psychological story: Once there was a town, and in that town lived people known as The Procrastinators. Naturally, they were known far and wide for all the things Procrastinators don't do, like arrive early for anything; have a calm and forthright demeanor; always radiate cheerfulness; rebuke themselves for their bad behavior. And, of course, they felt they didn't get a fair shake in life—others had advantages they deserved.

Interestingly enough, there was a man living in a nearby village that had heard the complaints of this sad lot of ne'er-do-wells for so long that he decided to put them to a test and give them a chance to help themselves. Also, he knew there were people who wrongly felt sorry for The Procrastinators. Their living conditions were terrible, all because of them being the way they were. The man was very wealthy and he felt compassion for his fellow man, so he decided to put his plan into action.

Soon the word spread amongst The Procrastinators: a train was to arrive in town at 3 a.m. on the 5th of March. The train was to take any and all that wanted to leave their dismal home to a new home in a far away beautiful, clean village. Each was to be given everything needed to make a new start for their self once they arrived.

The 5th of March came and went. Only one man boarded the train for a new life. He was given a new home, clothes, furniture, and funds to make a fresh start. He lived happily ever after. What happened to the rest of the people? Well true to form, they procrastinated. And still true to form, complained that the hour was too early, and that they should be given another chance—and all the other things The Procrastinators usually say. End of story.

Never feel sorry for anyone. If there was a magic pill available that would put an end to one's problems, most people would not take it.

** See questions and answers 10 and 16.

Affection

It has only been in recent years that you see young people displaying their affection toward one another and smooching in public. It is really not affection at all, but simply an act to try to convince themselves and others that they are special—that they have something no one else has. First, something Truly Special never needs to be confirmed. Only something false trying to pass itself off as authentic needs confirmation. Next, real affection has no opposite—it never turns into anger, or feeling hurt, jealousy, or negativity. That is the test that the validity of all feelings should be judged by: Does it ever change into something else? If it does, it is an impostor—a lie.

** See question and answer 25.

Nosy

People are nosy and they love to gossip. Just because someone asks you a question doesn't mean you must answer it or explain why you choose not to answer the question. Never answer a question you do not want to answer. Try this: Change the subject by asking the questioner a personal question. It works most of the time. People love to talk about themselves.

** See question and answer 27.

Problems

Believe it or not, we love to have problems. Why? As long as we have problems and, therefore, something to complain about, we feel real and alive. As we confront one problem after another, it also gives us a false feeling of accomplishment and of going somewhere in time. We think having problems proves we're working at life in a positive way. Nothing could be further from the Truth. We love problems because they keep things so messed up, so distorted, that we can't see a very simple fact: You and I, we are the only problem we have. When one discovers the true source of all one's problems, there are no more problems to solve.

** See questions and answers 18 and 28.

Sick

Self-centered people love to get attention any way they can. One trick they use is to mentally make themselves physically ill—a psychosomatic sickness. Be strong. Don't buy into the act. It hurts all concerned.

** See question and answer 1.

Attachments

People get wrongly attached to people and things. Notice how some people worship other people and/or possessions. They equate it with security. In reality, it causes them worry and anxiety. They constantly fear they might lose whatever they are attached to. A very wise man once proclaimed, "Love the Creator, not the creations." That's sage advice.

** See question and answer 20.

Belief

Try to take people's beliefs away from them and you'll have a huge fight on your hands. Strange, isn't it? We so easily take beliefs as facts that we soon completely forget the difference between the two. The next thing you know, we'll go into the fires of hell to defend a belief. But why? It's so painful. We're terrified of not knowing. We wrongly believe the pain we endure defending our beliefs proves we're right. But, the truth is, all it proves is that we're causing ourselves a lot of pain. Look, why do we need beliefs at all? What's so bad about just sticking to the facts we know and acknowledging the things we don't know? Then we can inquire and discover new facts.

** See questions and answers 8, 16, and 19.

44

Loyalty

People can have unnatural loyalties to self-defeating behaviors. The next time you meet an unhappy person, try suggesting that they simply give up the hurtful feelings and then watch their reaction. You would think you were asking the person to give up all their valuable possessions. It would benefit us all to regularly reevaluate our loyalties.

** See questions and answers 12 and 22.

Time

When it comes to the concept of time, let's discuss two kinds of people. There are those who say, "There's plenty of time, I'll do it later." And there are those who say, "Just not enough time, I'm really feeling the stress." It's best not to fall for either of these tricks of wrong thinking. There is actually no such thing as psychological time. We use clock time as an agreed-upon convenience. In reality, there is only the eternal "now." All reactions to time are self-induced. Please ponder this seriously so you'll not suffer again from the unnecessary pain of creating psychological time with your mind.

** See questions and answers 7 and 11.

46

Good

Our society would have you believe that you can become good through what it pronounces as "good deeds." Or to put it another way, something that isn't good can somehow do good. Doesn't make much sense, does it? Why? Because you can't get pure water out of a tainted well. Of course people want to believe otherwise, because doing the "good" prescribed by society is so very easy as opposed to the hard work required to be Good. As long as one has hatred, violence, greed, lust, etc., in one's heart, no good can come of it. When one purges oneself of all that is not decent in one's heart, then every action is Good naturally. Yes, you can do it—it takes unrelenting, vigorous, tough self-honesty.

** See questions and answers 2 and 9.

Excuses

Please verify this for yourself: Watch any person as they make an excuse for their bad behavior. Are they not placing a heavy brick on their own back? The brick of insuring they will do it all again—including the self-induced pain. Never buy into people's excuses for their actions. There's only one reason people do what they do—they want to!

** See questions and answers 4 and 26.

Solutions

The world has organizations of every type to supposedly help overcome life's problems. Each group proclaims their solution as the definitive solution. Don't believe it. There is only one True solution for our universal problems: each of us must see that we, individually, are the problem—not the solution. When one sees oneself as the problem, the problem vanishes.

** See question and answer 5.

Fairness

Some cry out for fairness. There is no need to seek fairness. Life is fair. We are all born with an equal responsibility. The responsibility to become nothing more and nothing less than a truly decent human being. Then, and only then, can you be fair.

** See question and answer 24.

50

Meaning

Many people seek the meaning of life. Others claim to know the meaning of life: acquiring money, sex, having a beautiful body, traveling, family, love, serving others—you name it. Some even say life has no meaning. Of course, the reason people believe what they believe about life's meaning is to soothe their agitation over not really understanding life at all. Their false belief comforts them. Don't fall for any of these nonsensical explanations. Look around you. Watch people when they do not know they are being watched—when the social mask is off. You'll have a difficult time finding anybody who looks happy. Most people, especially the older people, look very unhappy. Sure, on the surface people can look happy. Be sure to look deeply—look through the facade.

To properly discuss the meaning of life one must first distinguish between life, with a small

"l," and Life, with a capital "L." Most people are content with life with the small "l": a life of drudgery, despair, fear, and searching for temporary comforts while projecting an image of understanding, strength, and security. Plus, is it not arrogant of us to think that we must give a meaning to life? Does not Life, of itself, have intrinsic meaning? Only when you give up all the false pursuits of a life with the small "l," can one enter into Life with a big "L." At this level of spiritual development, you and Life are not separate—there is only your nice, new Life— "you" and life have merged. How? Because you saw through the illusion that there ever was a separate "you." Then Life reveals and expresses its meaning willingly. Then reading people (including "you") is like second nature.

   ** See question and answer 22.

A Revealing Question and Answer Session from a Class in Corvallis, Oregon

1.
In your book you talk about the importance of a person's inner environment and that someone with a depressed spirit should be avoided as they could darken yours. But is it possible for me to help such people by surrounding them with my cheerfulness?

Look, if we were all psychically wide awake it would be different. But we're students working on ourselves, so we can't waste the energy. In our present state, we are trying to rise above the world's hypnotic state; we can't afford to lose the energy by being around people who want to drag us down and drain us. Energy is very, very important. We need the energy to be alert and to be aware. Awareness is energy.

2.

In the book you talk about the events in our lives, how they are determined by what our nature is, and that anyone can change their life anytime they choose by simply changing their nature. So we have to just look at our nature factually, good or bad, right? I know I don't want to see what's bad about me.

Yes. But let's look at it a different way. What's wrong about our nature doesn't want to see what's wrong about our nature. And the problem is that we think that is *us*. That is, we are identified with the dark part of our nature. But we are *not* that. We think we are, because we are so used to having it around. Anything we are used to and is familiar to us, we identify with. Especially what's inside of us. We think it's my personal self, my personal possession— so I want to protect it. This can get me in trouble—having a nature like that. Consequently, it is good for me not to go along with that, and to expose it for what it really is, so there can be more of what I really am.

But, the dark part of our nature doesn't like it. It doesn't like it?—So what!—Do it anyway!

3.

Does everyone have a hidden motive, or are there some who are "nice people"?

In one part of the New Testament, people are talking about Christ being good. And Christ rebukes them, saying, "Why do you call me good? None is good but God." We can say it this way: only niceness is nice. There are no nice people. But also, do you understand that there's not the opposite either? We don't want to label people nice or not nice. We're using the examples in the book to point out that there are a lot of people trying to pass themselves off as something they are not. We want to watch out for that type of behavior, both outside ourselves and inside. We want to see where we are pretending to be something we are not, so we can then express the niceness that is given to us from above. I can't create niceness; I'm not the creator of anything.

4.

Your book puts fifty types of people in a kind of lineup and shines the bright light on them—or us. It then becomes clear that nobody is what they seem to be. We're all trying to appear to be something we're not. Right?

Yes. Everybody is pretending to be the "self-picture" they have of themselves. And the proof of that is, if you psychologically step on somebody's corn, then they'll let you see what they are really like. And then people say they are only like that because somebody did that to them. But, as I've said many times, a beautiful fawn doesn't turn into a raging hyena! You can't change into what you are not. What life is all about is seeing that I am pretending, and that I'm covering up things about myself that I don't want to be exposed. By exposing these things, the light will dispel it, then I will naturally be what it was always intended for me to be. Then I won't have to pretend about anything, because it is just natural. We all feel the anxiety, the split, of trying to pretend to be something we're not. Yet if we all acted out what we are actually like, it would be a lot worse than it is! But again, I want to stress that in essence we are none of that. And that the meaning of life is to rid ourselves of that which we are not. But first I have to see through my own act.

5.
When I see the truth about myself, I will want more of it?

Right. You could say it another way—the more you can take, the more you are given.

I want to be clear, though. This is not something I'm making up. This is all fact. And anybody can prove it for themselves.

6.

If I fall for the acts the people in your book are playing, I'm fooled twice! Once by them and then by my reactions. For example, if someone deceives me I'll feel bad.

There is never a right reason for feeling bad. But on the other hand, I want to see when I am inwardly going awry. I want to be very much aware of that so I can self-correct. But feeling bad is just another mistake. And the reason we feel bad is because it fits the image we have of ourselves as being good people, and good people must feel bad in order to show they're good! How about not feeling bad, and just not do whatever it was again? And what good does feeling bad do? How does it help anything?

7.

At some point you need to make a stand?

Yes, I have to make a stand—against what is trying to convince me (and has done a pretty good job) that I have to have a miserable life and that I need to just pretend that I have a good life. When I take a stand against that, it will all fall apart. Then I can have a nice life, and I don't have to pretend.

8.

In the book, you bring up the subject of carrying unnecessary baggage. How can I have a nice life when I'm carrying around all this old luggage full of useless reactions?

Some friends and I went out into the high woods recently to cut firewood. Do you know why people like to do that? Because you don't take your baggage up there. It's pure manual labor, and you put your image down for a little while. Your baggage is your image—all the things you think you know, all the things you believe in. But up there in the hills you're just a novice, and everyone knows that; they're novices, too. So you don't need all that luggage and you can have fun! Only problem is, then you become an expert and the fun goes out of it!

9.

My favorite story in this book is the one about the sheep on the hillside and how the sheep all end up with rings in their noses, thinking they are individuals. Can society as a whole move in another higher direction, rather than decline as it is today?

Wouldn't it be nice if the world would turn around and be nice? I'm afraid the evidence shows that the world is not going to do that. But that doesn't mean that anybody who wants to can't do it. Anybody who wants to can travel the higher road. That doesn't mean though that you should feel superior to those who do not, nor that you should condemn them. That would be self-righteous. What we're saying is that you just feel the need in your heart to not go along with what the world is selling. You want something different, you want something higher. And you shouldn't proselytize and talk other people into it, because all you'd do is stir up trouble. If people want to join you on your journey, fine; if they don't, that's fine, too. It's their lives, just like it's your life.

10.

Are you saying that most people don't want to change, even though they ask you for help?

Yes. Remember the old saying, "Talk is cheap." It fits here.

11.

I was looking through the book and came to the chapter called Relax. It was so refreshing to realize that I could relax and not be so tense.

Right. It's a human trait to put off things like relaxing until we're through making ourselves a wreck. And we say that we make ourselves a wreck so that we can relax later! We could just relax now, and that would be the end of the whole business. But our present nature doesn't like that. If you are sincere and conscientious, you should be able to relax. The wrong parts of us say that if you are sincere and conscientious, you have to have pain.

12.

I felt a little shame when I was reading the part in your book about the couple that drank the pure water in the oasis while the others went on in the wrong direction. It made me stop and realize that I am going in the wrong direction.

It's so easy to go in the wrong direction. And we must never condemn ourselves when we catch ourselves in the wrong direction. In fact, we should be jubilant, because before, we didn't know we were going the wrong way.

13.

Mrs. So-Nice lives next door, and she's always coming over to borrow a cup of sugar or to give me something. I want to tell her that I like my privacy, but she's so nice I'm afraid to say anything to her.

It's a funny thing about all of us, because somehow we got the idea from our parents or from others that it's wrong just to have your own life or to want your privacy. We feel that it's wrong to say to someone, "Excuse me, but I'm right in the middle of something right now." We have an image of how we have to behave. Of course you don't want to be tactless; you want to be tactful. But, sometimes you have to be pretty firm with people, because they can be hard to get through to. But if you just excuse yourself in a nice way, tell them you're busy and need to take care of something, the other person will get the idea and eventually not come over so often. If your mind begins to torment you and say that you treated them badly, you can see through that, because that's just a trick.

14.

Whenever I go visit my relatives, I leave feeling dragged down. I feel obligated to go and guilty if I don't.

I'm not in the advice-giving business. I'm not Dear Abby. What I do is tell people what they need to hear, so that then they can do for themselves what they need to do. And all anybody needs, myself included, is to do the most important thing that any human being can do—wake up. We need to become what it means to be a real human being; to get rid of all the ideas I have about who or what I have to be, all of that kind of thing. Then I can just be natural, and truly be one with the universe. Then, the things like the problems with the family will not be problems for you at all. It will be so easy and so casual for you to do the right thing. So put first things first. Do that, and then none of those things will be a problem for you.

15.

You talk about negative feelings that we have and not giving into them, bearing them consciously. Can you expand on that a little more and tie it in to accountability to ourselves and to God?

I like the word accountability, because it's rare that any of us ever stops long enough to be grateful that we were given a life. We are always so interested in wanting more, that we seldom stop to be grateful. We are always worried about what we didn't get, instead of being thankful for what we already have. That's very, very important— that we have a sense of gratitude. But we also should have a sense of indebtedness. That it's not a free ride; that we owe something back. And what we owe back is that we will all work on ourselves to become truly decent human beings. Then, in doing that, the negativity becomes something very different. We can use it to go higher and higher up the higher road. We can use it as a tool. We understand the negativity, and so the more of it that we can rid ourselves of, the more we can catch that is still there. So this working on myself constantly is an ongoing project. And that is how I pay off my debt—to the universe, to God, however you want to call it—for having a life. For having been given a life.

16.

I get excited when I read this book; I've read it several times. And I get all charged up and ready to go out and do things and be different, but somehow I always lose my momentum and fall back into my usual ways.

First of all, it's a natural thing that we start out with some excitement, and then the resistance comes. You just have to remember that you will be inspired again. What you need to do is just keep walking, no matter how difficult it is, just keep walking. Then you'll see that you get through it, and you're energized again, and you'll have the enthusiasm to go right ahead. You take ten steps forward and fall back nine. But that's okay, you're still making progress.

17.

One of your uncommon tips states that there's never a time to feel sad. But I feel that way a lot. Somehow I decide that?

Right. You can choose not to be sad, even though there are parts of you that insist on it. Maybe there's even a part of you that wants to feel sad, and is feeling sad, but you do not have to go along with it. Once the sadness sees that it can't play that trick on you anymore, it will leave you alone. It'll find a new "sucker."

18.

It seems few people, even so-called spiritual students, ever get to the point of choosing not to feel sad.

Something that I have discovered in my own inner spiritual work is that the last thing people want to give up is their suffering. We're so convinced that we can't be a good person if we don't suffer. And about that image of being a good person: first of all, I found out I didn't have the slightest idea what a good person is or was. All I had were ideas I had made up or other people had given me. Ideas are not reality. Thinking I'm a good person doesn't make me a good person.

19.

If I didn't have ideas about being a nice person, what would I do? I wouldn't know how to act.

Do you think that the birds outside the window have ideas about how to act? Aren't they just pure birds? They don't have a problem. They're just natural. So when you don't have ideas about how to act, that's good, because then you'll be natural—you won't be acting! We're all afraid to enter into the unknown because the known holds onto us and says, "You're going to get hurt if you leave me." Go ahead and leave it, and you'll see that naturalness is just waiting for you. That's why it's so nice to watch little children, puppies, and kittens because they're so natural. Why should you need to know how to act? That presupposes there's no naturalness.

20.

The prospect of changing myself makes me feel a loss.

A very wise man once said that if you can lose it, let it go—it's better to lose it sooner than later!

21.

If you have to convince yourself you're a good person, you'll also have to be a victim, right?

Right. There's a part of being a "good person" that means, for one thing, that you let people take advantage of you. Then you become a victim. Don't be a good person; don't be a bad person. Be no one. In reality you are no one. You truly are one with the Whole—one with the universe. That's a fact. We're not separate. We don't have a separate self. And anyone who wants to can know that can feel it and live it.

22.

At the end of your book, you discuss the meaning of life. You seem to say that we can reach a point where we don't need to be self-protective or wary anymore, but just be aware of what's going on inwardly and outwardly. Is that a different level we can reach?

Yes, that's when a person sees through all of the labels they have ascribed to themselves and others and understands that there is no such thing as a separate self. They know they are not separate from other people; they are just part of the Whole. And from that point on, everything is different. Everything is just natural for that person. There is no need for any of the things that people who have not reached that level depend on. It's the state all true mystics describe. For instance, Christ called it the Kingdom of Heaven within; Moses described it as the Promised Land; Buddha called it Nirvana.

23.

You've said sometimes we have to play a role consciously.

Yes, at work or somewhere where you have to consciously do what is necessary, because there are people there who would not understand such things as working on oneself. So you might indicate you have an interest in something you don't—say, some civic problem—in order to be sociable or get certain things done that need to be done. You are being consciously sociable.

24.

I notice that you handle all sorts of people and situations very nicely—for example, putting other people at ease. This seems like a higher and nicer state.

Yes, and it's a natural part of self-development that comes from rigorous inner work. And then, it truly is a gift from Above. It is not something, though, that any person creates for themselves. It is something that is given to them. Human beings are not creators. Even when a scientist makes a discovery, he didn't create the brain, the breath, the heartbeat—so, did he make the discovery, or did just part of the Whole discover something that was always there?

25.

It's terrible to feel special, isn't it? We think it's good, but it's really bad. If I want to be special, and then people don't treat me the way I think they should, I get upset.

If you want to be special, you'd better have some of those little cards with a $20 bill attached that you hand to people that says, "Treat me special!" Being special is just another one of those labels. It's hell trying to convince everybody that you're special, because they want everybody to feel that *they* are special. So you have a clash of specials. When you think about it, it's all absurd. Our psychology needs a good sorting out, and you can do it. The fact is, there is nobody there to be special. Our imagination has created this separate self, and as long as you're separate, you can't be in harmony. Everybody longs to feel they are part of something, but they can't because they are "separate." But this is only in their own minds and that can be cleared up. There is a longing inside of people to want to be completed. It's a longing to go home. What does it mean to go home? It means to become Whole, not to be divided, not to live the kind of life we have all lived, and to be at peace while we're here in a physical body. Anybody can do it. That's home. We are running away from what we need to run toward, and running toward what we need to run away from. We have it all backwards.

26.
You say in your book, "Don't do as others do."

Right. Thoreau said, "I march to the beat of a different drummer." He did not do as others did. We all wrongly believe we too march to the beat of a different drummer. The fact is, most of what we do, think, say, and feel, we picked up from others or inherited. It is very difficult to free oneself from this acquired mechanical behavior, but it can be done. To be sure, doing just that is an integral part of the meaning of life.

27.

We need other people, difficult people, in order to grow, right? That's the way out?

Yes. My mind says that the other person is the problem. Obviously that can't be true because if that person really is irritating, he must be irritating to everyone, which he is not. Also, the same thing that irritates me when that person is around, also irritates me when I am alone! The only way to be free is understanding all of this and using it properly. Staying right in the middle of it, until the understanding dawns. You can't get it with your mind; you have to live it. You have to use the pain of the situation to teach you the lesson it wants to teach you. And the lesson it wants to teach you is that it is stupid to be in pain.

28.

The problems we have been discussing seem different at first glance, but I wonder if they really are?

It's all just pain. If we sternly refuse to buy into the pain, then healing can come. How? How does my body heal itself from a sore or an injury? We don't know how. It just happens when the conditions are right. We need to invite the right conditions psychologically and spiritually by not doing what we always do. Then the healing comes. You can count on it!

About the Author

Murray Oxman is a bestselling author, seminar leader, and psychological researcher. He has been featured on radio and TV shows and in newspapers throughout the country. He's published in the prestigious *American Journal of Psychology*. In over twenty years Murray has led thousands of classes and seminars.

He emphatically says he is not telling anyone what to do, either in his writings or talks. He is only saying what he has learned the hard way, by self-observation and being ruthlessly honest with himself. Murray lives and teaches classes in Corvallis, Oregon.

To contact Murray Oxman or for information about classes in Corvallis, Oregon, please write or call:

Success Without Stress
5445 NW Crescent Valley Dr
Corvallis, Oregon 97330
541.752.0870